Thanks!

Mildred W. McKinney

A STAIRWAY TO THE SKY

A STAIRWAY TO THE SKY

MILDRED W. McKINNEY

A Lyceum Book

Carlton Press, Inc. *New York, N.Y.*

Manufactured in the United States of America
ISBN 0-8062-0852-X

CONTENTS

AMERICA

A land of beauty, deep and wide,
A land where Faith and Love abide,
A land where Right confronts the wrong,
A land that thrives on prayers and songs,

A land of grain, timber, and ore,
Cattle, cotton, factories, more,
A land that huddles wandering sheep,
A land that loves and laughs and weeps!

I love this land: this land of love
And share her Woes with God above.
I hail her virtues, loathe her vices.
God, PLEASE forgive not once, but thrice!

GOD HALLOW THIS USA

Dear God, Hallow this USA
Whose lady hurls her torch afar,
Unfurled banner whispers: "Sweet Peace,"
Her bell shouts limpid: "Liberty pays!"

She hails depressed, desolate hearts:
Her ambered beauty molds a light
For those who search to sip the Right,
Accept each hail and take a part.

Her mountains stand with outstretched hands;
Her plains spurt grain from each nip'd breast
And hail hale hands trembling with zest
As roaring billows give commands.

Dear God, protect that gleaming torch
Keep wheat for bread, songs for orch.
God bless our dear old USA,
Hold her feet in that righteous way.

WIN ROCK

Win, Rock
Did call a tax legislature;
But, Rock,
He wanted tax of no nature!

Knock, Rock
And turn the third term big wish knob!
Why, Rock?
To spread a better rich man's job.

Three knocks
For better prisons and top schools
Hear, Rock:
"This can't be done by the work of fools!"

AMERICA, MY COUNTRY

America, America, America, America!
In colors Red, White, and Blue
With hills that kiss the trees afar
A heart of love, it's big and true.

America, America, America, America!
With hands like iron you grip the poor,
With legs like steel you walk in pairs
And strive to heal all dripping sores.

America, America, America, America!
Your stars and stripes, your torch so bright
Give strength to souls both near and far
And hurl some thoughts from wrong to right.

America, America, America, America!
God sees your work and knows your heart.
So keep your mind above the stars,
Let liberty proclaim each start!

HAPPY BIRTHDAY, AMERICA

Born of hearts with valor true,
Shaped solid in marter so pure,
Nurtured in wisdom firm, secure,
Grew from impotence to mature.

At ONE, she earned that gleaming torch;
And heaved character taut, unscorch'd.
Her unfurl'd beauty veiled that orch,
Compassion tall stood on her porch.

She's grown, now, she's pregnant with love;
She's strong, now, sucks milk from above.
Two centuries old, still meek as doves.
Her highest goal? To birth more love!

I KNOW THIS IS SPRING

Though traces of dull winter stand,
The paint of spring colors the land.
Heartbeats of trees awake the grass
Violets peep as brisk breezes pass.

Desolate forest're stuffed with music
Tumbling from birds, brooks, and breezes;
Golden sunlight warms each meadow,
Silver raindrops make way for grain.

Frangrances of spring make burdens light;
Sunrays of spring make paths so bright.
Music of spring turns wrong minds right;
Blossoms of spring says: "Love's in sight!"

THE BEAUTY OF AUTUMN

It's autumn, now!
The leaves are sipping amber down;
The grass is snatching up deep brown,
Squirrels stuffed with nuts are hollow bound.

It's autumn, now!
Cornstalks have bowed their fingered heads;
Acorn shells've popped, berries're red,
The bees have stored their winter bread.

It's autumn, now!
The days draw short, the nights stretch long
The geese sail South, North Wind hums songs,
Chilled dew whispers: "Soul, march on!"

It's autumn, now!
My silver locks flop like thin lace;
My crumbling limbs have pierced my pace,
Time's ploughed furrers in my tired face.

At autumn time,
Life's sorrows tell such pensive tales
Hate, Greed, and Strife bundle in bales;
And tears like raindrops burst life's hale.

It's autumn, Lord!
Though friends are few, my thanks to You!
Dark nights hurl strength for Life's great task,
A calm winter is all I, now, ask.

WONDERS OF AUTUMN

Autumn's breathing,
All grain's sneezing;
Amber's blazing,
Nature's amazing!
Autumn's swallowing Summer's meat.

Rose-fingered clouds're streaking the Dawn,
Brown spreads her blanket on the lawn.
Mice await the ripening corn;
Squirrels sneak, snatch, and crack acorns.
Autumn smells winter's breath!

Cottonstalks drop their crispy leaves,
Nude cane lies curled in massive heaps
Autumn yields pay for Spring's toils,
All life depends upon the soil!
Autumn unfolds the secrets of Spring.

Autumn's breathing,
Nature's heaving!
Winter's creeping
Souls are reaping!
Autumn reveals the toils of Life.

THE SIGNS OF AUTUMN

Autumn,
Ambered forests blanket the earth.
Autumn, Autumn!
Pumpkins swell and beckon the frost.
Autumn, Autumn, Autumn!
Sun sleeps late and hurries to bed.
Autumn, Autumn, Autumn, Autumn!
Both the Dawn and Dusk breathe chilled, frosty air.

Autumn,
Nuts are falling, brooks are shrinking.
Autumn, Autumn!
Iron-grey pillows float in the sky.
Autumn, Autumn, Autumn!
West, milky clouds hop orange and red.
Autumn, Autumn, Autumn, Autumn!
Melancholy feathers deck each bowed head.

Autumn,
Patience boldly meets the morn!
Autumn, Autumn!
Beauty brightly the universe paints.
Autumn, Autumn, Autumn!
Diligence whispers, "Come, now, rest."
Autumn, Autumn, Autumn, Autumn!
Nature's Love's seeking for her fellowman!

Autumn!
This pregnant Earth gives birth to food!
Autumn, Autumn,
Earth's dripping breasts beg to be milked!
Autumn, Autumn, Autumn,
Earth's silent lips crave kisses hot.
Autumn, Autumn, Autumn, Autumn!
God's wisdom teaches man, the End is nigh.

IT'S WINTER NOW!

It's winter now, grey curtains hang afar
Towering above the peaks of ice-caked hills
Well draped with messages warm and profound,
Trembling with great fear of North Wind's rude breath.

The silent sky breaks windows through the clouds;
Bare trees, shivering, sigh and grey heads bow.
Animals smell smoke towering from aloof,
Snowflakes form fleecy blankets on each roof.

Tightly frozen are the doors of kindness;
Icy and slippery are paths of Joy;
Chilled are the winding stairways that soothe Pain.
It's Winter, now, beneath it lies the Spring!

JOYS OF WINTER

Return, Dear Winter Hour!
Grey mornings yearn your breath;
Rooftops beckon your white flurries,
Elms and Oaks have shed their gowns.

Hail Thou, Dear Winter Hour!
Harvest from meadows awaits the cows,
Barns stuffed with fodder, oats, and corn
Will nourish the steer with sawed-off horns!

Hurrah! Dear Winter Hour!
The Earth now smells your blizzard breath;
Whirling snowflakes now deck the roofs,
Elms and Oaks have bowed their grey heads.

Hello! Dear Winter Hour!
Souls born and worked in early spring
Mature in silent summer sun.
Those reaped and stored in autumn hours
Walk securely on Winter's Ice!

A SALUTATION

Good morning, Sir, I marvel you!
I saw you from my window when
You split the shadow of the dawn.
You look'd so tranquil in your grin;
Then pok'd rays through to all your men!

I heard you lapping dew from grass;
I saw you suck it from the leaves,
I heard you laugh with your sly pace,
I thought you'd crack your pretty face!

Are you always glad when the clouds
Hide your face from the roaring crowds?
Or, do you prefer that the day
Be bright so you can have your way?

Were you ever a baby chap
Who had to coo on Mother's lap?
Or did you leap from world unknown
All big, stocky, and all full grown?

You're always so gay and so bright,
You must sleep mighty well each night.
Do you drink your milk with a grin?
I've ne'er seen any on your chin.

Good evening, Sir, are you tired too?
You've grinned, you've danced the whole day through!
You've shared your beauty strong and bright;
You've shown the lost the way of right.
If I were big and strong like you,
I'd pierce the world with wonders too!

HELLO MOON

I like watching you lean from sky
And kiss the trees there standing by.
I hear you tell the flow'rs and grass
That you're just a lump of gass.

Where are you during the long day
When I'm allowed to run and play?
I believe I could hear you laugh
If I didn't watch you through this glass.

Why are you sometime big and long
And other times you're round and strong?
Why do you, sometime, sigh at dusk
And times, at dawn, you grin at us?

Sir, I like your cloak of yellow
And think you're a lucky fellow!
Why you don't have to bathe at night
Nor say prayers when you fight!

If I, like you, could chat with wind,
I'd punch the world beneath her chin;
Then I'd hide in some secret place
And watch you laugh and split your face.

FLOWERS

Abstruse ladies luring in frocks white, blue,
Spotted flaring frocks of amber and red
How do you stand that chilly morning dew
Dripping over your fluffy, blooming head?

You, your bright beauty thrust upon the Earth,
All ugliness beneath the vast tides fling;
But when you shed your showy evening dress
Your flairy Gaiety is moaned worldwide.

Lead on, Dear Ladies, sow your proud power
Until you Earth thrusts from her chilly breast,
Just keep brazing this gloomy path of ours
Till you God ushers to that couch of rest.

VEGETABLES

Onions're arayed in blade green tops,
Beets in imperil red.
Cabbage wear dark green and some white,
Magnificent when they're headed!

Beans leap in bunches, on wire, poles,
All okra crawls in pods,
But serves no purpose when too hard:
Unlike crisp leaves of green Swiss chard!

Since these dear plants sustain sweet life,
Why should they go to seed?
They never sin, yet, they must die
To meet demands of sinful needs.

THE EFFICACIOUS WIND

I like to watch when you slap trees
And their branches you spread about.
Fun it is to hear your sweet breeze
As well as your strong angry shouts!

Why do you sometime nip our nose
And, sometime soothe our scorching feet?
Why do you sometime bite the toes
And sometime rock the baffled soul?

You whip the world with such wonders
That no born man has pow'r to match;
Oft'n when I should be slumbering,
Such wonders plague my nonpluss'd wit.

If I, like you, could smite the world,
I'd flog indolence and unkind;
I'd swipe all slums in one big whirl,
Swallow illiteracy in time!

But you smile as you pass it by;
Snore while ignorance lashes the poor,
You refuse abuse of power.
Allow unrighteousness to score.

THAT LAST TOLL FOR ME

Twas a morning stuffed with sunshine;
Highways widened to cars sublime.
The distant trees all bowed their heads,
And buzzing bees ceased baking bread.

The flowers sprinkled frangrance sweet;
Echoes of frogs and crows did meet.
Billowing brooks roared loud and deep,
And newborn chicks cried PEEP, PEEP, PEEP!

A morning crambed with feelings strange;
Fate held great tidings for the sane.
Doom smiled on thoughts that pricked the lame;
Hope stood in silence o'er his cane.

The school stood tall with sagging jaws;
Children like frogs leaped through the halls
Teachers in awe awaited calls,
Their minds jumped back to early fall.

Stood *one* afar so bright, so fair
Who'd climbed that ardent flight of stairs,
And, now, breathed frozen, parting air.
Yes, soon there'd be a vacant chair.
The bell tolled loud and clear and free;
That teacher wept where all could see:
"Wail not, comarades! Drink deep and BE!
I hail that bell's last toll for me!"

A TEACHER

Unlike the stern sour pickle
One she is who all keeps tickle;
Not with futile-filled jokes that harm;
But bold firmness, knowledge that warms.

Shows she courage that hues the path
And kindness that turns sobs to laughs.
Stands she as tall as any wall,
Implores all children to her call.

Tough as cud her patience stands,
Grasping, tenderly, for each hand.
Loud as a lion her kindness roars;
She sifts Compassion as she soars;

Teacher? One she is who hath all this
Regard for Time and heartfelt Bliss,
Tolerance, Meekness of a lamb,
Accepts she me for what I am!

WHY?

Why load me with tons of sorrow
As I tug along Life's dim way?
Is it because days are borrowed,
I've just one chance to pass this way?

Oft I'm plagued with sharp disaster
That knocks me on my knees to pray.
Still cling I that I may answer
When He my name calls on that Day.

I wonder why I'm pitched and tossed
While trying to do the Master's will?
Why dumped on me such heavy cross
While I fear to temptation yield?

Why do transgressing, sinful lives
snatch happiness from my sad eyes?
Please teach me how to sacrifice
And leave my problems all to Christ!

SOME PEOPLE

Some people howl the queerest things,
They utter words that truly sting!
They bark when strangers pass them by,
And strive to gnaw the stars from sky.

In winter, they growl: "It's too cold!"
And oft abuse they the great Fold
During summer, they roar: "How hot!"
And frown when the sun yells: "I'm not!"

Like cows they low when snow blankets the earth;
Like horses they neigh when flow'rs kiss the birds.
Like pigs they squeal when taxes go up;
Like frogs they hop when caught in ruts.

Zoom they and cackle when all's well;
But moan like doves when bills give them hell!
They paddle and crawl when the path is dark,
Coo and caw when caught with bad hearts.

Some people? Oh, they are the funniest things!
When paths are rough, how they can pray and sing!
When paths are smooth, such LITTLE time for pray'r;
But growl and nourish like grizzly bears!

THAT MISSING SPARK

Met I a lad along my way
As I approached the close of day.
He said he'd longed to trod that path
Where Knowledge seeds are thickly sowed.
But had he not that proper pass!

He talked of schools, teachers and books;
He knew of bees, wild beast and brooks;
But dropped his head in mighty shame
When I, too, asked from whence he came.
He'd rather not that story tell.

His twinkling eyes, then, warmed my heart,
I wondered if I'd done my part.
Had I sought to stake needy out
And spread some love and hope about?
I heard my dull heart cry: "What shame!"

I watched that lad trodding along,
Soothing his woes with his own song.
Then turned and crept along my way.
But to each step my heart did say,
"Compassion shown with love you've not!"

I swirled and sought to catch that lad,
But only found my journey sad.
When one has missed some part of life,
His heart is filled with Hate and Strife.
Then, turn our way? He just may not!

A BOOK EXHORTATION

Read I a book the other day,
It told of people far away.
And on each page found I a thought
that hurled my woes and whims awrought.

Blabbed each sentence, calmly, to mee:
"There's much in this wide world to see!
And there is so much each child here can learn
If he the right to read can earn."

Pressing the pages of that book,
The world I gave one tranquil look.
Thought I a thought, another thought
Of the many books that are sought.

Thought I of those who are in need,
That boy, that girl who cannot read.
If they but had a searching mind,
What joy in books they, too, would find!

In pain, I read another book
Exploring each corner and nook.
And here, I found a guiding light
For those who blunder in the night.

Good books afford great joy for all,
Be either his world large or small.
Good books will help one find the way,
They break the darkness with the day!

MOTHER'S BIBLE

You blessed, blessed holy book
Smiling from your soft, cozy nook!
I like to snatch your sagging jaws
And learn of punishments that claw

When man refuses Thou mighty will
And takes his pleasure cup to fill.
I like to thumb your crispy leaves
And learn of deeds that merit sheaves.

You spurred my mother every day;
You kept her in that narrow way.
Wilt Thou: Dear Blessed Holy Book
Forever keep my mother's look?

IN SORROW'S POOL

For every mile I walked to school,
For every time announced a fool,
For every tear in Sorrow's Pool,
I gave my heart rewarding tools:

Courage to stand each ardent trial,
Patience to hear the smallest child,
Knowledge to know the truly wise,
Wisdom to refrain from disguise.

Tolerance to endure great pain,
Grit to fail and begin again,
Compassion to share all rain,
And love to touch the wasted brain.

For every mile I walked to school
I found, for life, a worthy tool;
I smile when I'm announced a fool
Because there's joy in Sorrow's Pool!

IF I WERE A MOTHER

Were I a mother in a time
like this
Always, I'd greet my family with
a kiss,
And claw my children with a will
to serve
When squealed they over troubles of
this world.

I'd stab the issues of these changing
times
And serve the dishes of the olden
style;
I'd prescribe looking the world in
the face,
Demand that each child digest Nature's
grace.

Were I a mother in a day
like this
I'd growl until indolence was dismissed;
I'd pierce my children with the wonders of
good books,
And beg the stars to kiss the roaring
brooks!

PENSIVE SOULS

Souls that observe the morning star,
The sun, the wind that hurl afar
Drink inspiration from above
Baffle hate with gentle love.

Souls that see wonders in the trees,
Dolence in the buzzing honeybees
Smell frangrances of mighty flow'rs,
Subdue cruelty with divine pow'r.

Souls that ponder the fate of life,
Untruthfulness, envy, and strife
Suck goodness from the breasts of God,
Find not His path too hard to trod!

AN APPEAL FOR RESTORATION

Mighty thou art, I admit,
Endowed with immense pow'r and wit.
You've pow'r to build and destroy
Material pleasures for human joys.

Dominion o'er this earth was toss'd to you
By one: a mystery yet kind and true.
You' with your yearn, ability to think
Have allowed morality to dive, sink.

Can't you see that it's time to pray
For baffling souls who've gone astray?
Let's stop and think for pity's sake,
Return to God 'fore it's too late!

I HAVE THE KEY

Having drunk the milk of sorrow,
Eaten that tough crust of solitude,
Felt those horrible stripes of hate,
And smelled the useful yeast of Faith,
I can smile when trouble stabs me;
I can float on clouds of danger;
I can swim the pool that scorns;
And I can climb that mountain of fear.

Life is made of rain and sunshine,
Valor, courage, disappointments.
He who lives it, must face hazzards,
Love man, trust God, obey His will!

Sorrow gives life strength and courage;
Solitude leads one to prayer;
Hate makes one determined to stand,
And strong Faith begets Fortitude!
A combination of it all
Gives life a key to all tough walls.

MY SECRET POWER

When my heart is weighty and laden
And my soul is both sad and sore,
Commune I with Mother Nature;
Tosses she my burdens ashore.

Hail I that crimson setting sun,
I watch the birds fly home to rest.
Listen I to bees that hum
As Nature huddles them with zest.

Way above that crimson sunset
Glitters that peaceful star, sublime!
That star that smiles and will not let
Sin disturb the truly divine.

Just shouts my spirit, then, with joy;
My soul, then, leaps to Peace and glows
With infinite, eternal joy
From that celestial stream that flows!

WORDS TO THE WISE

Fret not when thorns of Vice prick your kind heart;
He who made you sustains during dark hours.
Yield not to Vice, Virtue has greater pow'r!
He who made you shaped and set you apart!

Drink not that advertising milk of Hate:
Prepare not in your heart that bed of Strife.
Hail not termites of bad deeds in this life;
Lest Hell, afterwards, shall become your Fate!

Liberty proclaims him whom Nature prizes;
Budding trees, screeching owls hold healing power.
There's strength in croaking frogs and fragrant flowers!
Great purpose dwells in hearts of Nature's size.

Is not Man that wise beast that God made last
And gave dominion over both Sea and Grass?
How, then, can he be more rude than bees?
He's free and he's alone, God gave the key!

Return Dear Beast, use Nature for your guide;
Our Master frowns when we give way to Vice.
Virtue's much lighter, hails not once, but thrice!
Accept God's goodness, on His soft breast ride!

COME OUT OF THAT MELANCHOLY CLOSET

Come out of that melancholy closet!
Nature, for you, holds great glittering joy;
Her eloquent beauty holds sympathy
That glides to heal each broken, dripping heart.
With joy, each life the thought of Death must meet
And smile as Time approaches close of Day.

When, like ocean tides, sorrow floods the heart,
Blankets of agony the body shrouds,
Hide not thyself from nature's compassion!
Rather, suck her warm milk, nibble her crust;
Strength there is in all our God has made,
Nature all sorrow heals when she communes.

Life with none on silver platter sojourns!
It's a mixture of bliss, courage, despair
That ties Time's wisdom, fortitude and grit.
So come out of that melancholy closet,
Boldy drink Life's bitter desperations;
Fate holds tranquility beneath deep frowns.

Golden sunrays prick agony and pain;
Yellow moonlight splits the deep, heavy gloom
Budding trees, buzzing bees erase despair;
Silent moves of butterflies soothe all fear,
Roaring brooks, chirping birds make music clear,
Melancholy closets breed only grief!

A PROFOUND CONCERN

With every drop of rain that falls
And every breeze that blows
With every human need that calls,
My love for life just grows and flows!

A CONSOLING MESSAGE

May you, during this hour's sorrow,
Look forward to a brighter tomorrow
Because you're trusting God above
Who comforts man because He loves.

A GRATEFUL EXPRESSION

Accept my thanks to you
For things it took special effort to do.
Your visits, gifts, flowers, calls, and cards;
Your blood, your money all warmed our hearts

You've been just great in every way!
And for each deed allow me to say
Thanks to you in a very special way!

SOLICITUDE

I'm so sorry that you're ill;
But please remember God loves you still.
When you submit His will be done,
You, then, will concede your battle won.

AN HEROIC QUATRAIN

In spite of multi-narrow, rugged snares,
He sought to reach that distant, brighter star.
Refusing to succumb to boring stares
His crown now glitters, free from doubtful scars.

A MEMORIUM

Oh, days of yesteryears
That lend immortal light,
We, now, lament your bright light
To free mankind of fears.

AN APPEAL TO MAN

Will you please look to God above?
He'll touch you with His wand of love.
He knows; He sees; and He, too, cares
Give Him your burden and He'll share.

WORDS TO A FALLING FLOWER

These words won't make you well, I know
But will cheer you and let you know
that if *I* really had *my* way,
I'd make you well this very DAY!